High Cash Flow

Real Estate Investing

Learn The Secrets To Creating Hassle-Free Profitable Cash Flows In Real Estate Investing

I0492361

Written By:

A Cleveland Real Estate Investor

Valleywide Real Estate Investments

BOOK ONE

High Cash Flow

Rental Property Investing:

Getting The Best Return On Your Money In Small Low Cost Residential Rental Properties That Cost Under $99,000.

"Our 8 Keys To Successful Profitable Cash Flow"

"How To Invest Your Money

Into **<u>HIGH</u> Cash-Flowing** Rental Properties Successfully and **<u>With The Least Hassles</u>!** BY Following **<u>8 Keys To Success</u> To Be A** *<u>PROFITABLE</u>* **Landlord"**

"Investing Your Money DIRECTLY Into Income-Producing Real Estate <u>FAR Exceeds Traditional Investments</u>."

This small apartment house generates $1,050 a month, cost $46,000 and creates an annual return of over 25% for the investor.

Legal Disclaimer

Information contained in this guide is for educational purposes only. Always verify information against your local laws and conditions. During the investment property buying process, it is wise to have professional legal help of an attorney skilled in real estate law local to the property. This guide is not meant to take the place of professional one-to-one advice, but only to complement such advice. The information in this guide is the opinion of the author.

AUTHOR'S NOTE:

This book was written by an "In-The-Trenches" Cleveland-Ohio real estate investor and nothing here is candy-coated, nor should it be. You will get the truth about this business and what is necessary to activate the formula for wealth in cash flow properties.

If you question whether this business is lucrative, please consider that currently there are thousands of millionaire investors, groups, funds and billion dollar REIT's that are on a mission to accumulate and buy as much apartments and rental housing as they can get their hands on right now in this economy.

Residential rental property has never been stronger for many reasons. Get your share of this wealth while the "rental boom" is still here.

A 14-unit apartment building that cash flows $4,800 per month in Cleveland, Ohio and cost 75,000.

8 Keys To Success

Table of Contents

Direct Real Estate Investment

What is a direct real estate investment?

"Directly purchasing investment real estate in which you own and control it 100%. There are no money-managers playing with your money and you are not subject to volatile market forces and government influences, such as with the Stock Market."

Do you have money in any of the following investment vehicles?

- *Self-directed IRA Account*
- *IRA Account*
- *401K account*
- *Stocks, bonds*
- *Cash savings account*
- *Gold, Silver coins*
- *Physical cash?*

Is your capital earning you at least 15%-18% consistently in any of these traditional investments? How about 50%? 180%? If not, then you are missing out on great opportunities that will not be here for much longer! I will show you how in a moment:

We are now living in an economy that now requires the average investor to be RADICAL in his/her methods for preserving and growing wealth. This is due to the many changes that are occurring and will only accelerate into the near future as our governments fail to handle the Debt and economy problems in an efficient manner.

Although stocks, bonds and mutual funds would seem to be a very safe investment, they really are not. We live in digital age where our economy can have major distortions in the matter of minutes. Your INTANGIBLE stock, bond, T-note or 401K retirement account can very possibly disappear in less than one day if stocks become volatile enough. What about bank failures? Do we, the average American people, really know what is going to happen in our future or which banks will still be in business?

Why not invest your money in a proven system that has survived thousands of years, civilizations and can be dated back the Medieval times when the Feudal system form of government was the lay of the Land?

I am talking about the old fashioned hard asset called HOUSING, actual real estate.

There are certain types of real estate that are performing VERY WELL right now and always have been. Affordable apartments and housing are in great demand because people will always need a place to live. Business can go out of business and leave office buildings and shopping centers vacant, but well positioned residential real estate will never go out of style!!!

What's really great is that this certain type of housing gets stronger as the Economy gets worse, but it stays the same if the economy explodes or grows! Either way you can't lose. The key to any business venture is to have a product in which there is a strong demand for. If you can provide a quality product at a good price you will make good profits, very simple.

A large triplex that cash flows $1,250 per month in Cleveland, Ohio

When you directly invest in real estate you get the following benefits:

- Direct ownership to a solid tangible hard asset
- Title to land
- A valuable commodity that cannot lose value in hours or days in the same manner that a stock does.
- Can produce consistent returns with none of the volatility that stocks and metals offer
- Depreciation for tax write-offs
- Capital gains.
- Consistent positive cash flow.
- A bankable asset.
- Real equity not paper equity like stocks.
- 100% control over your investment – YOU determine if you gain or lose value on your investment!
- No "shady" money-managers.
- You can't lose your investment if you purchase the right way!

When you invest in the financial markets (stocks, 401K's..) you get the following in comparison to real estate:

- Intangible investment
- Rapid price movement
- Volatility
- Political and governmental price manipulation
- Very reactive to market fear and panic
- High taxes and no depreciation on your gains
- High capital gains tax
- Your investment is subject to strict regulation and control
- Banks could fail unexpectedly and you could lose your investment
- THE MARKETS ARE RIGGED.

There are markets in the U.S. that offer properties at such low prices you can achieve 15-35% returns from cash flow. Most people think that there must be some catch or that those cheap properties are only in war zones where no one else will go.

Well I can say honestly that that is NOT the case if you know the local market and how to find the hidden diamonds, **because in this current real estate market, when you find diamonds, they are BIG diamonds!**

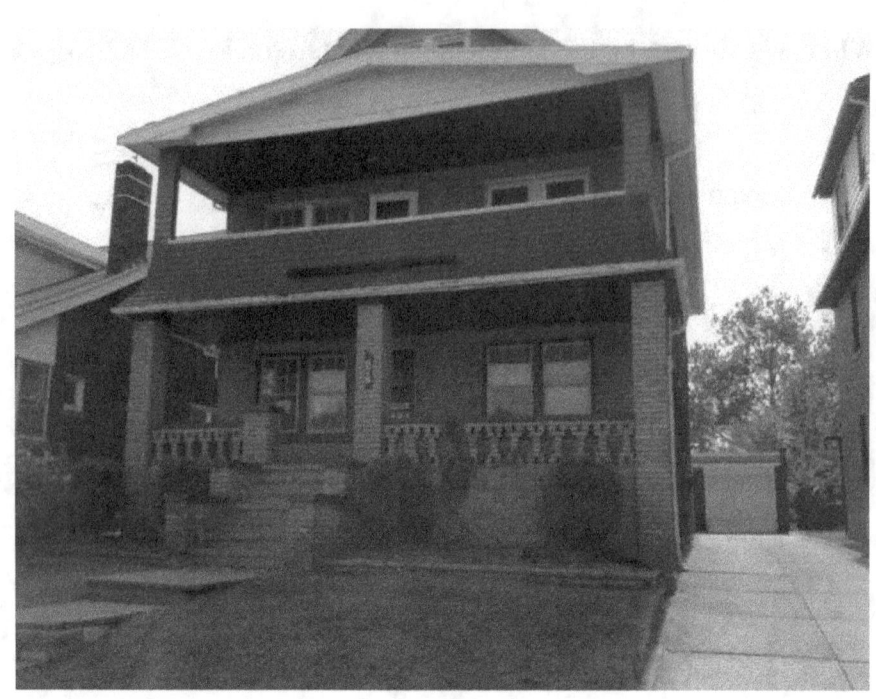

A huge, all brick duplex that cash flow $1,200 a month in Cleveland, Ohio.

I have invested in real estate in war zones, and have made excellent returns and margins there, but I knew what I was doing. The key to those areas is fast action, in and out; rehab and lease fast and have security systems in place.

So eliminate any fears you have that those high returns come with horrible nightmares because they don't. Some investors that I talk to simply don't believe me and decide to settle for less returns, for example, he/she will purchase a newer construction turnkey rental property for $100,000 in a sunbelt market and make a 10% return on their capital investment. ***I'm sorry, but a 9-10% return from rental income does not even make me the least bit excited, in fact it makes me depressed to settle for that little return!***

That's great if it is ok with you, but please remember that the chance of a significant general run-up in home values anytime in the next 10 years is most unlikely. We will be lucky if the residential market values merely stabilize, and that will only happen if the foreclosure rates drop significantly and people start buying and financing houses like crazy again. **Thus far, the best trend to date is affordable rental properties that cash flow positively!**

A pair of run-down bank-owned duplexes I picked up for $11,000 each. I rehabbed and leased them. They are now cash-flowing over $2,200 per month. (This is the before rehab picture)

Your Local Market

One of the most important keys to success in this business is to know your local playing field very well. It is the oldest rule of thumb in real estate and is more important now than ever before.

Years ago you could buy a house anywhere and make all sorts of mistakes and still make money, now you cannot do that, you have little pockets of good fundamentals out of a whole city or region, then you have other pockets that are just terrible places for renting or selling and you must avoid them.

That's why starting in your backyard is the best way to go, you already know the area and have access to contacts and can view properties right away yourself.

If you don't like your local market where you live and want a cheaper, better investment market, you will need to have the following elements in place before investing there.

Local Teams

You must have a team in place with the following team players: A reliable contractor, subs, handyman, lawn maintenance, legal contacts, agents, information, etc. Align yourself with an investment expert such as a successful local full time investor.

You will also need to familiarize yourself with the following local market trends:

- Market Values (Not ZILLOW values or appraisals)
- Rental rates
- Rental demand
- Political environment for investors/Landlords
- Section 8, if interested
- Other state-assisted rent programs
- City inspection procedures, if any
- Rental permits, if any
- Rental tax, if any
- Dead zones
- War zones
- Middle zones
- Transitional neighborhoods
- Suburbs
- NSP neighborhoods
- Community development corporations

The bottom line is you must have a local team when investing from out of the area. It is very unwise to simply purchase investment property yourself through an agent you never met and plan to manage it yourself over the Internet. More of this is explained in the management key success chapter.

An All brick duplex that cash flows

$1,050 per month in Cleveland Ohio and cost $45,000.

Absentee Or Local Ownership

A local investment plan is the best situation to be in as you have fast access to your property, tenants, vendors, contractors, deals, etc, etc.

However, since the Internet Revolution, anyone can now view properties online and gather all necessary information over the phone and websites. There is only one ingredient missing when you are absentee that cannot be done versus a local owner, and that is; your "sixth sense" when dealing with people.

I used to like to meet my tenants to get a sixth sense for what they were all about. It's something that comes with experience. I generally always meet contractors, as they are renown for ripping investors off. I can usually spot a scammer fairly fast these days.

You can be very successful as an absentee owner if you follow a specific protocol in your dealings and management systems and have a local team in place. There is a way to set up a virtual system whereby you don't even have to ever meet or speak to your tenants and they never know you even exist. Once again, this is only possible if you have the proper LOCAL team and SYSTEMS in place.

If you are doing everything yourself, finding deals, rehabbing and marketing and renting, then being "In the trenches" is the best way to go, **however if you are buying turnkey, investment grade cash flow properties using service providers or investment**

professionals who do this for a career/living, then you can live where you want and invest where it makes sense.

Most investors opt for the turnkey investment package, as that has the lowest risk, cash flow from day one and doesn't have to involve the investor in a risky rehab or lease-up.

There are professionals that do this full time for investors that desire a turnkey situation, and are still able to offer a cash-flowing quality investment property yielding a 20-30% return annually.

Management or "Bandagement"

Management is a very important topic, especially for long-distance investors.

Here is a statement that will surprise most of new investors: **Most of the professional licensed management companies out there are some of the worst managers and many are crooks.** Not ALL are that way, but most usually are. How can I say this? Because I have been through it over and over and most of them only want big commercial accounts, but will say "yes" to small income houses and apartments because they reason that SOME money is better than none, but they never do anything but waste everyone's time!

Now don't get me wrong, I understand how difficult management is and how much work is involved, <u>but a high integrity management company should turn down business they won't be able to effectively handle.</u>

In order to keep your investments cash flowing positively for a long time you need strong management. **"Bandagement" will not work.**

Let me give you some ideas on management

Self-Manage

Some inexperienced owners elect to self-manage, which often turns into bandagement once they realize they aren't doing things right and have lost too much money, they start to put repairs off and eventually become slum lords or walk away from the whole business with disgust and conclude that there is no money to be made in real estate.

Do not self-manage unless you are local, experienced or your tenants have agreed to perform some of the basic duties of a property manager.

Professional licensed manager or company

This can be a real estate broker that has undertaken management services for additional fee and income or a fully committed management company, but very rarely is the firm specializing in just management. Problem is, most of them take on too many houses and properties and then they can't effectively manage time sensitive matters and needs. If you are not a major client, you should expect "blow-offs" and bad service, which costs YOU money.

Professionals like the apartment buildings and big income properties, but they just can't say no to houses and apartment houses. So they contract them and then can't perform thus wasting everyone's time and money, or even worse; they lie and steal from you.

The "Chop Shop" Manager

This is usually an un-licensed manager, or perhaps an agent, but they are usually undercapitalized, a sole business owner running their own show. Somehow they got into the business by agreeing to look after a few rentals, perhaps originally a contractor, tradesman, etc. However they got started, they figured they could make good money with 10, 20, 50 houses and by doing any repair work that comes up as well. Some of them eventually figure out they can steal rent money and over charge for their repairs and rehabs.

They talk a big talk and say they can do a lot, but in the end, it's all a scam for your money. **Not ALL are like this but most are** and there will be warning signs up; front which we will discuss here shortly.

The Small "Custodial" Manager or Maintenance Manager

This is the best form of management for 1-10 small income properties. It is simply an individual that is very familiar with the neighborhoods, knows vendors and contractors, is a handyman himself, and is very available, personable and reliable.

This is also the typical in-house maintenance person many owners of 25-50 unit apartment buildings typically have living in one unit for free or reduced rent. Typically this guy shows units, performs the minor maintenance items that you never even hear about, is on top of what is going on, regularly drives by your properties and **establishes and keeps rapport with your tenants.**

When you find someone like this, consider yourself VERY lucky; this is exactly the type of management that works for small income in the 1-50 unit range.

Typical red flags and tips to be aware of when dealing with management companies and chop shops:

- If they own their own properties, they will place the best tenants in their rentals. Stay away from managers that own their own portfolio in same market.
- Never answers the phone or returns your call same day.
- They keep coming up with repairs needed for your property
- Their marketing strategy is flimsy sign in your yard
- They aren't placing ads specific to your property
- They ask for fee money upfront
- They don't perform a background check on tenants
- Their management contract favors them only, leaving you out in the cold in the event of a dispute
- Too slow in responding to your calls
- They do it all…such as contracting, sales, broker, investing..
- They are investors acting as managers, which can be a dangerous mix.
- They don't know the subsidy programs or procedures in the area
- Bad leads management, such as, when prospective tenants call they just get an answering machine over and over and no one ever calls them back.
- The manager does not even live in the market or lives in another city, need I even say anything more on this one?

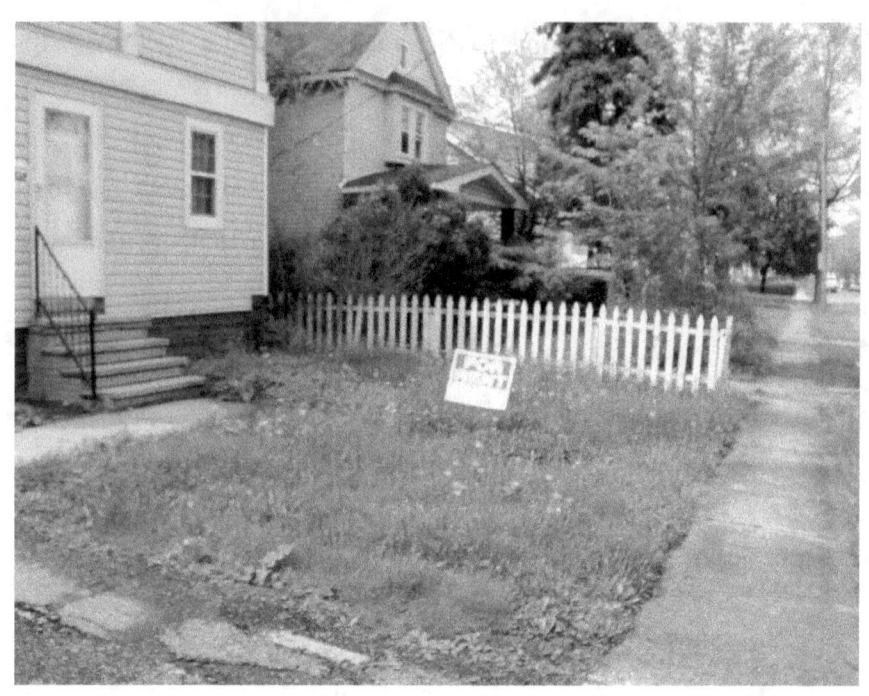

Here's an example of bad management and a cheap generic-looking For Rent Sign. Notice the neglected lawn. This is what a lot of inefficient managers do. This is what attracts "bad" tenants!

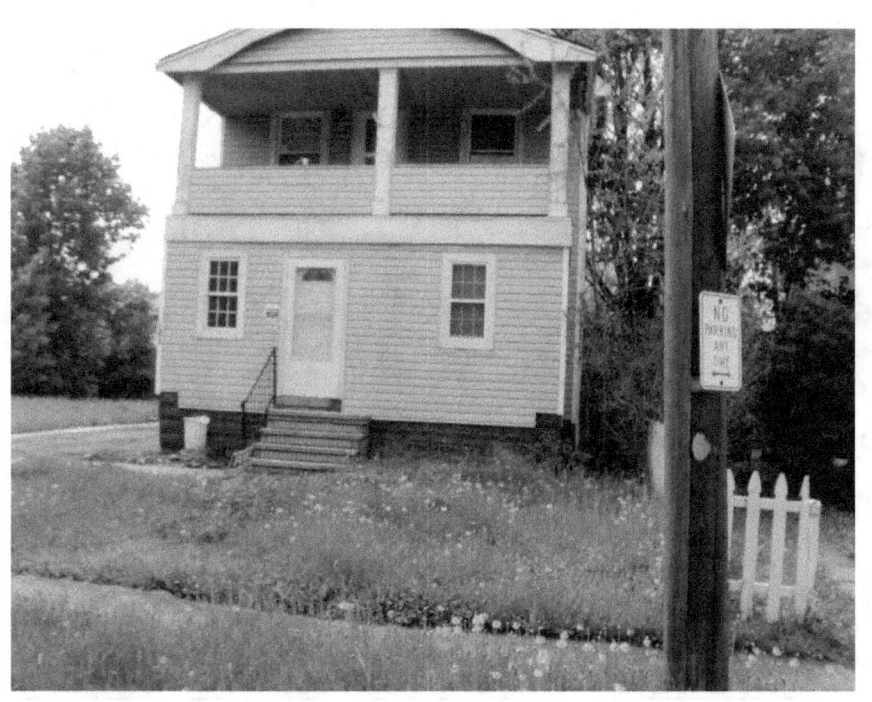

..More Bad management. Same house.

Neglected lawn maintenance due to more bad management

An example of a simple well-managed lawn, which any serious management company should do.

What kind of fees to expect:

Professionals charge typically 10% monthly gross for 1-4 unit residential and for the placement fee they get one month's rent on move-in date.

For larger properties is varies from 2-5% of the monthly gross and flat leasing commission for new apartments rented.

Chop Shops will sometimes try to get more.

Small maintenance in-house type of managers will normally get 10% or a little more but believe me it is well worth it.

Common methods dishonest managers use to steal money:

They claim they have a vacancy but upon your inspection the unit is occupied, which means the manager is pocketing the rent money, pretty simple.

There is only one way to eliminate the risk of unaccountable theft, and that is to have the tenant direct deposit the rent money into your bank account. Put the responsibility on your tenant; eliminate any type of 3rd party rent collection.

All of my tenants go to a chase bank branch on the first of the month and deposit CASH into my rental account. There is no one else involved, Thus, if a rental payment isn't received, I know it's because the tenant defaulted, not because my manager swindled me.

In conclusion, based on my experience in buying, rehabbing, leasing and selling over 70 apartment houses in Cleveland, I have learned what works and doesn't work too well for small residential income properties

What typically works?

- Small custodial type of manager
- Lives in the neighborhood or area
- Runs a small operation
- Has vendor connections and is a handy-person
- Personable business relationship and direct contact

What typically doesn't work for small income properties?

- Large management firm
- Large coverage area
- Has a large management volume
- You feel like just a number
- The management firm also owns rental properties in same market.
- No personable attention or service
- You can never get them on the phone
- Everything takes a long time to do
- Accountability factor is low
- They make you sign their ridiculous contract that favors them only and allows them to fire YOU if you get on their nerves.

Maintenance and Repairs

Investing and owning real estate rentals is NOT like owning stocks or bonds. You are dealing with an asset that actually exists in space-time. This asset is subject to the forces of nature and time. This is why you have depreciation and other beneficial write-offs.

Deferred maintenance is absolutely unavoidable and ANYONE that ever tries to sell you an investment property and says it needs no deferred maintenance is either a liar or a fool. Even turnkey rentals will need some maintenance here and now. Deferred maintenance can be anywhere from a $20 fix to a $500 fix. It all depends on what condition the property is in, what is updated and outdated, good tenants or bad tenants, the age of the property, etc.

They key to minimizing your deferred maintenance cost is to invest in **quality rehabbed cash flow properties only and to screen your tenants.**

If you are doing the rehab yourself **do not cut corners, it will cost you twice as much down the road.**

Here is an example of a costly deferred maintenance item: <u>Exterior painting</u>. Notice the flaking paint. You could let it go, but it looks terrible and will affect the quality of tenant you attract. In Cleveland I can paint this entire house for only $2,000 materials and labor. It is well worth the expense to attract a quality tenant that will stay for several years and pay rent on time.

Items that need to be in good working condition:

- Roof
- Flooring
- Electrical
- Plumbing and water tanks
- Doors and windows function
- Lights
- Furnaces
- Paint
- Toilets and shower
- Plumbing fixtures, traps.
- Faucets

How to Screen Tenants

Your cash flow life is directly determined by the quality of the tenant that you place in your rental properties.

Most of the horror stories new investors read and hear about through second hand information are from landlords that have mortgages on their properties and need the money fast so they take the first applicant that gives them cash or money upfront, without doing proper income verifications, or background checks.

Most of us have made this mistake before.

The best way to screen your tenants, and make your life cash flow happy, is to follow the outlined protocol here:

- Get a fully filled out application with SS number and address, etc.
- Have a bullet-proof lease ready to go.
- Check their criminal history in every state if possible, if you don't want to pay for a vendor service, at least check in your state using the online clerk of court websites in all surrounding counties, also check the municipal clerk of courts.
- Acquire job income verification, 2-3 most recent paystubs.
- Get a copy of driver's license and cross reference the information with what provided on application.
- Any discrepancy in provided information with what you find in your checks is a red flag.
- Ensure they disclose any other adult occupants, and if so, they also must fill out an application and go through the same checks.

The main red flags you are looking for is:

- Unauthorized occupants (generally a female applicant is a "front" for a un-qualified male applicant/prospect)
- Convicted felons or criminal histories.
- Eviction history or currently in eviction.
- No income – non-verifiable income.
- Fake social security #'s

Instead of doing all of this yourself, you could hire a property management company to do it, but they charge money for the services they use, and in my experience, these 3rd party vendors OFTEN miss checks in the background. They simply will not do as thorough of a job if you did yourself, seriously consider this; taking the 1-2 hours to do a thorough check on an applicant can save you lots of money in legal fees, let alone the headache and trauma of dealing with a bad tenant

Most investors use a property manager to perform these duties but it's good to know how to do the checks yourself, which I highly recommend if you only have a couple rental properties.

Besides minimizing deferred maintenance, screening your tenants is KEY to long term cash flow with your cash flow properties. Finding the right tenant is a simple procedure anyone can do. By screening your tenant, you eliminate the often heard, stereotypical nightmare scenario every landlord knows.

The D.I.Y. Process

Have prospects fill out an application after they have viewed the unit. All requested information must be filled out. If they are leery about giving you their social security number or other personal information, like a drivers' license number; move on, they are hiding something.

A typical "rental area" type of street in Cleveland, Ohio. Grovewood Avenue, there are no cars parked on the street because everyone is working during the day, it's a blue-collar area and this is where you want to be investing in.

When doing your checks, you want to look for these red flags:

- Felony convictions
- Current or previous evictions
- Misspelled names, not using their legal names.
- Bad referral from 2nd previous landlord
- No job or employment income
- Too many occupants (Use HUD guidelines)
- Big pets such as large dogs
- Lied on the application
- Provided fake references
- Lawsuits or history of suing people, especially other landlords
- Criminal convictions or a history of crime
- Income too low (Use your established criteria)
- Partiers (Find out through other neighbors where they live now)

Exceptions that I generally overlook:

- Evictions more than 3-4 years ago.
- Felony convictions revolving around a domestic violence loophole or was manufactured by other party for vengeful reasons.
- Minor felony convictions over 10 years ago as long as it was NOT a violent crime such as; murder, robbery, aggravated burglary, arson, etc.

- Legitimate lawsuits.

- Recent foreclosure (very common several years ago)

- Bad credit from job loss or other uncontrollable circumstances.

To find most of this information for free, visit your County's online Clerk of Court dockets database. Be sure to check both **county** and **municipal** Clerks of Court records. This will reveal any current or prior civil and criminal cases within the area.

Otherwise, the verify everything in one paid shot, most background service checks cost $25-$50. To this day I merely check county and city docket websites to verify applicant's information.

A Large all brick triplex that cash flows $1,550 per month in Cleveland, Ohio.

How to Analyze Cash Flow

When looking at turnkey residential income properties for sale on the Internet, it's important to be aware of property related expenses.

Below are some common necessary costs in owning income property that is the same in most every city in America.

Property taxes

This varies greatly by city and county, some cities require a rental tax, others do not. All require you to pay property taxes. Most tax departments are allowing property owners to appeal their tax value assessment and have it reduced because of the Housing Decline. I did this in Cleveland and reduced several of my holdings assessed value by almost 30%

Water / Sewer / Garbage Collection / City Services

This expense can be the most annoying of all because it can fluctuate greatly depending on water usage by your tenants. Since most small income properties only have a master meter for water, it is the responsibility of the Owner to pay the bill. It is important to maintain a close grip on water usage when you have a master meter.

The only way to really do this is to constantly remind your tenants to conserve their water usage, limit the number of occupants per unit and put a special clause in your lease that states and abuse of water or overages will be billed back to the tenant.

Property Insurance

Insurance is an absolute necessity, however, I have accidently let some rental policies lapse only because I forgot about them. Before the housing bust, there were a lot of insurance underwriters and it was a very lax environment for rental policies. Currently you have only a few underwriters for rental housing left and they are somewhat strict. I pay about $30 to $70 per month for an individual policy on a typical apartment house but I do not insure for full replacement value or full market value.

For example, I have a brick triplex that costs $150,000 to replace and has a fair market value of $85,000. Let's say I am invested in the triplex rehab and cost of $50,000. I am only going to insure it for $65,000 because that's all I need in the event of a major catastrophe, I will get my cash investment back and a premium on top of that if I'm lucky. Never use insurance policies as a money-making venue, it merely protects your cost or investment in the event of a disaster.

Property Management

Management costs are optional but if you are out of the area and not able to check on your properties physically then you will want to use a qualified manager to run your properties.

In my experience, you are going to pay 10% of the gross or a flat fee depending on what kind of management person you are using.

Most insurance inspectors will threaten to cancel your rental policy of they see a minor roof repair such as this. This roof was not leaking, but they thought it was a risk to them. They give you the choice to repair it or the policy will lapse.

CLEVELAND OHIO!

Real Life Cash Flow Ledger:

A 3-unit apartment house in Cleveland, Ohio.

Purchase and rehab cost: **$43,000**

Rental Income

Unit 1	$550
Unit 2	$550
Unit 3	$300
Total	$1,400

Expenses:

Taxes	$154.22
Insurance	$55
Water/Sewer/Garbage	$68
Management	$100
Total:	$377.22

Cash Flow: **$1,022.78 Per month.**

Return On Investment: 29% (Annual net cash flow / Purchase and rehab cost)

So in the above property (One of my best properties) I am making about $12,000 a year free and clear on a 2-unit apartment house I own in Cleveland. I pay a little less in management because I have a long-term relationship with my "custodial" type manager.

Did you know that if you own 10 duplexes like the above one free and clear you will receive over $10,000 a month in net profit, or about $120,000 a year after all expenses?

In Cleveland, your cost per property shouldn't exceed $40,000 to $50,000 if you are doing the locating and rehabbing yourself. So as you can see, getting over 20% returns on your investment capital is VERY realistic and possible right now in certain markets…BUT NOT ALL. Sometimes I make 40% or more if it is a triplex or small apartment building, but that's a totally different scenario we'll cover later.

Duplex that cash flows over $1,200 a month in Cleveland, Ohio.

Turnkey Cash Flow Investing

It's time to talk about your goals as a real estate investor. Because there are so many books, courses, gurus and real estate "experts" out there claiming you can make easy money flipping houses, doing shorts, etc. it has caused many to have some very unrealistic expectations about this business.

Personally, when I started, I thought I could flip 10-20 houses a month and become a millionaire in Cleveland. No way, when I experienced how much work and detail goes into a flip, even in an UP market, that idea went out the door and into the garbage along with the courses I bought.

I eventually bought a course on buying and rehabbing apartments and making $10,000 a month with no involvement in operations and/or doing everything from remote control.

Another guru myth, don't believe the hype in those real estate courses out there! My first apartment house rehab deal took me 6 long months and everything that could have gone wrong did. Rehabbing is not easy and requires GREAT mental fortitude, systems and patience. What is really interesting is it takes just as much work and energy to rehab a 3-unit building as it does an 80-unit garden-style apartment complex.

So, if you plan on rehabbing, you must be prepared for the most risk. You also need to be in the market physically or have a team there that you can trust and has a track record.

If you do not like risk or can't tolerate unexpected overages, costs, mistakes, bad weather, contractor mistakes, etc, etc, then rehabbing is probably not for you, especially if you are going to try and do it all yourself from a great distance.

Advantages of buying turnkey rental property:

- Low risk
- Cash flow from day one
- Fresh rehab and tenants
- Low deferred maintenance
- No rehab
- Anyone can invest in them, no specialized skills needed.
- Higher returns when leverage is used
- Very manageable to own from long distances

Buying rehab properties

- High risk
- You get more equity
- Requires specialized skills
- Organized team necessary
- Cost over runs
- Very difficult to do long distance

Opportunities in affordable housing and apartments are only going to explode in the next few years because of the following trends:

- Lack of apartment supply and high demand
- Less homeowners, more people want to rent
- The Millennials are in their prime renting age
- Stable and rising rental rates
- More families being displaced due to never-ending foreclosures

Don't miss the wave, apartments and rental housing is shining right now. But, like anything else, nothing ever stays the same, and who knows how long this will last before things change or interest rates rise.

Low cost rental housing investments also carry these benefits

- Recession-proof
- A great shelter against Inflation

- Depreciation write-offs
- There are always renters and always will be
- Solid asset that no one can take away from you (unless you don't pay your taxes)

Questions?

Call today for a free consultation, I've helped many investors succeed.

Dana Onyshko

https://www.valleywideinvestments.com

www.ValleywideInvestments.com
(216) 220-7027

BOOK TWO

High Cash Flow

Rental Property Investing

Getting The Best Return On Your Money With The Least Hassles In Rental Properties That Cost Under $99,000.

"Real Life Tips & Traps Included"

Valleywide Real Estate Investments

Written by an "In-The-Trenches"

Cleveland, Ohio Real Estate Investor-Operator.

Legal Disclaimer::

Introduction:

I started out investing in low to moderate-income apartment houses and single-family homes. Based on my experience, this kind of investing has the best cash flow and wealth building potential the fastest in this current economy. But there are rules to this game, like any other business.

As an experienced full time real estate investor in Cleveland, I get asked a lot of questions regarding residential investment properties. However, what I always notice is most new investors don't seem to be getting "real life" information that is so critically important to any local market. It is easy to find real estate courses out there that are great for showing the many ways to make money, but what about the *real life* events and issues that crop up and have the potential to wipe-out the investor's profit?

It's my goal to illuminate some key tips and traps of residential (1-4 units) real estate investing in this short e-book that I feel are very important, whether you are a "turnkey" cash flow investor or a rehabber. I am only briefly touching on these topics due to the very broad and large amounts of information it would take to truly cover everything from A to Z.

Table of Contents:

Chapter 1:

Market Insights

As I revise this book again in October of 2017, the housing market has returned to normal levels and many markets are in a strong Sellers' market, even Cleveland. The real estate entrepreneurs and investors that thrive in this kind of market will need to adjust their acquisition strategy from REO, MLS and Trustee/Sheriff sale to create marketing, networking campaigns and working with city development channels.

For instance, I am now sourcing most of my property deals from strategic targeted postcard and Google Adwords campaigns, whereas; up to 3 years ago all I had to do was go on the MLS and bid on REO properties which were EVERYWHERE.

I am now moving into networking with attorneys and probate / estate law offices because there are an incredible amount of estate deals in the Cleveland area market, or anywhere where a lot of "old" people reside and have owned their homes for over 20-30 years.

REO's? forget it, even when they do come on the market now they are mostly overpriced and they have the 20 day investor offer restriction (Only homeowners or governments can bid on them).

Many banks have been stalling, extending, sitting on property that is defaulted or foreclosed in the hopes of "riding out" the Recession. Although NO ONE really knows what our economic out-come will be or will look like in the next 2-5 years, we should prepare for the worst AND the best case scenario! How does one do that you may ask? Simple, buy as much low-cost positive cash flow income property as you can, if we experience rapid inflation and increased commodity costs, landlords win, if we experience major deflation or stagnation, smart landlords that purchased low cost rental properties with a positive cash flow also win. Either way the real estate cycles always repeat themselves, so eventually prices will come back up.

But the one thing to consider as a real estate investor going into the future, is that builders will probably not build enough homes to stay up with demand when the cycle returns, this will be due to the fact that material and labor costs will probably increase, and there may be a shortage of skilled labor too, as many millennials decide not to get into construction trades. This could cause the next up cycle to be quite strong, in addition to a shortage of inventory. To make matters even more inflationary in this prediction, if shortage is low, baby boomer home-owners are not going to sell, if they have no house or condo to move to.

"Change Is Certain & History Keeps Repeating Itself"

Long ago in December of 2006, I received a call from my trusted loan officer that the mortgage financial markets were in trouble and things were going to change drastically. A few loan programs were being cancelled and there was a bank called Lehman Brothers that was removing their stated income loan programs, and the rumor on the block was that they were in trouble (what an understatement that was, we all know what happened to them). In my opinion, things started getting shaky even before that, but unless you were in mortgage banking or in the trenches everyday full time, a builder, developer or commercial property owner, most people didn't catch on until late 2007.

So, not all real estate investors knew or heeded this at that time, many of my associates and investors I knew of locally kept right on buying low and rehabbing with the expectation that they will be able to do a 80% refinance or retail sale after repairs and rehab. Many of those investors did refinance into 1,2 or 3 year arms and then lost their properties to foreclosure. Some paid cash and couldn't sell so they rented them out, some used commercial or home equity lines of credit, which got called in and they couldn't pay. Some had used hard money at

18% interest with the expectation of selling within 3 months from purchase and rehab. They didn't sell because the market changed and RETAIL prices went down, end-buyers couldn't get purchase loans anymore and a foreclosure wave hit many major markets diluting values across the board.

At that time, I was selling refurbished and wholesale Cleveland properties to investors in multiple states. Basically, anyone that was priced out of an expensive market that had negative cash flows would look into the Midwest and Northeast markets where cash flow and equity has always been abundant.

Many of the investors wanted cheap fixer uppers and were using Realtors to source contractors and property managers, who were not always looking out for the investor's best interest and most of these investors had no knowledge of the local neighborhoods. They had no local team and no contacts from the beginning.

The most common mistake I see new or out-of-area investors make is overpaying for repairs and buying the wrong property, or buying the right property at the wrong price, or a mix of everything. I have also made this mistake several times in the past.

In my opinion, you have to buy the right deal, at the right price, with minimal repairs in order to achieve a good rehab budget and profit margin, so that you can get a great tenant in there or sell it and make a profit in a market where everyone now expects a discount and values have reset..

Another common mistake I see new investors make is overpaying or getting scammed by a contractor.

It's also the one most feared by most new investors, but there are ways you can protect yourself and hold them (contractors) accountable. The biggest one is an investor paying 50% or more down on a job. I've even seen some investors put the whole amount down in advance! Well, you know what happens; the contractor ripped the investor off. "Why would someone pay in advance?" you may ask? Because they just want to trust someone and think they are going to make fast and easy money, even in today's market. I go over these strategies in the Chapter on contractors.

Into 2007, 2008 and 2009 foreclosures became so rampant that banks started selling blocks of houses to one buyer. The Cleveland area was a common ground for that. I had the pleasure of seeing and talking to a few investors from other markets that came in, bought 50, 100 even 200 properties in my local market in one transaction. Average purchase prices about $500 to $2,000 each house.

Then, they would sell them on terms with a small down payment. Most of them were garbage houses and garbage deals.

Many were demolished by the city or condemned. Most of those portfolio buyers just wanted to flip the house at a $1-5K mark up to some poor chap that has no idea the taxes are $10,000 delinquent, title is clouded and there is a major list of violations on the property and they City is putting the property on its "grass cutting" list, which they then charge $500 per cut. Eventually, most of those buyers walked away and the City demolished the house!

Towards the end of 2009 many of the REO inventories started easing up a little due to the banks "extend and pretend" and loan modification policies, of which the U.S. government is involved in mostly. Because of this, we now see quite a large "ghost REO inventory" accumulating in certain markets and areas (this does not apply to all markets).

I decided to pursue more quality properties and not even bother with questionable deals or small properties, due to the eroding fundamentals just starting to show. Into 2007 things didn't change much, loans were still getting done, stated income loans, low doc, etc. Then Bear Stearns and Lehman went under. Now things started changing. Some of my associates that had done very well in flipping houses from 2001 to 2006, decided commercial real estate was the next best thing, thus leaving the residential markets. I have always kept a very conservative investment strategy. I avoided debt and used my own cash reserve to purchase and renovate. When I started

I did have a passive partner that accepted a 10% return on his money, which I used to buy, refurbish and sell or wholesale Cleveland properties. Eventually I built up a cash reserve and no longer needed a private money partner.

Chapter 2

Common Myths

Myth#1: Passive Rental Cash Flow "Effortlessly"

There is no such thing as "effortless" passive real estate cash flow.

It's a myth that gurus created to inspire unseasoned and new investors to buy their book or course on the idea that they can buy properties and get checks in their mailbox of several thousands of dollars per month with minimal effort or no effort at all.

As an experienced investor from the Cleveland, Ohio real estate market, I quickly learned long ago that was a big myth in many ways. But believe me, in the beginning when I first started, I was sold on the idea of making $10,000 net cash flow per month passively like clockwork with no involvement in operations.

Buying profitable residential and apartment properties will require work, lots of hard work. It doesn't matter if it is a small 2 family property or a 100-unit apartment building, to receive and maintain a positive cash flow will require you to work at it often and keep on the DETAILS very often.

Now once you have a system in place, managing cash flow becomes a routine and you get used to doing the things to ensure your cash flow continues, then it's not work anymore, it's just new habits that have been formed in your life, so you get used to it and hopefully is fun for you. That's the point that takes work to get to, about 6 months to a year for un-seasoned investors (Based on my observations), depending on your desire, commitment and goals of course.

Real estate is a very broad, all-encompassing entrepreneurial field of business that can appeal to many different personalities and characters. There are so many different types of property classes and investment techniques that I truly believe anyone could find a niche somewhere in this wonderful business whether it's in owning a parking garage or sitting on a cheap affordable duplex in Cleveland that is generating over $13,800 per year in cash flow.

If you are new, the key is to find your niche and leverage it all the way. Some investors will be long-term landlords, rehabbers, intermediaries or apartment building investors. You may discover land lording is not for you and you really want to sell and cash out over and over (Flip

Emphasis: Be willing to work hard and manage your team.

The Fear Myth: Don't buy into fear and panic - buy into great deals:

I got started in real estate investing when mortgages and sales were fluid and easy. There were a lot of investors in the market, not very many REO's or foreclosures, and where they came up there was a lot of competition on them, yes, even in Cleveland. (Remember, Cleveland is not a very big town, its population is around 430,000, but was originally built to house around a million people in the 1930's to 1950's.) I saw a lot of people doing a lot of deals, flipping, renting, refinancing and cashing out over and over. After 2007, one by one they started disappearing, every year I noticed more and more investors leaving the scene and better, cheaper and more profitable quality distress deals coming onto the market as each year wore on into the housing decline.

My advertising responses are usually a good indicator of the market. In 2003 and 2004 when I started, I used to place good, large ads in the main newspaper, and it would fetch around 250 calls. In the summer of 2005 and 2006 my ads were pulling in 20 calls a day from buyer/investors. In mid-2009 and late 2009, I was getting around 2 calls a week from my ads. However, the quality of the retail buyer was much, much higher. Some were paying all cash, had excellent jobs and credit, etc.

One of the greatest times to profit in the real estate business is when others are in fear and panic mode, or when the news media is screaming that house values are falling and the market is bad. I'm sure you heard Warren Buffet stated somewhere, "be greedy when everyone else is scared." The motivated sellers will be everywhere and you will cherry-pick the best ones of course. It's great because if you are dealing with an unreasonable seller, simply walk away, they will sometimes get nervous and then want to deal with you, trust me. The fear and hysteria will not last though; it never does, no matter how bad it seems, until the banking system collapses or the Dollar is debased, the cycle will always come back.

I recall in late 2008 and January of 2009 many of my associates were scared, looking to sell their holdings and get out. It was so unreasonable. I'm talking about apartment owners, and investors that had 50-100 houses and apartment buildings. The stock market crashed, people lost their portfolio values, and every news channel was talking about the mess and what would happen if the entire financial system collapsed. The media took people on a major roller coaster ride.

In January 2009 I picked up a Fannie Mae-owned triplex for $14,000. It was all brick, 3,100 square feet, concrete paved driveway, huge 4-car all brick garage, rear parking lot huge basement, 2 BD per unit, large units, with fireplaces. It was located on a very nice street of Cleveland. The cost to rehab it was $15,000. I sold it to a cash flow investor at a 40% discount of it's fair market value. I gave the investor a GREAT deal! He has a positive cash flow of over $550 per month and a 4% - 30 year fixed loan. The property is truly worth around $125,000.

The worst things became in terms of frightened investors and foreclosures, the better deals I found which meant I could deliver better cash flows and equity to investors.

I found the best properties right when the housing collapse started in 2007-2008 and into 2009. I was even purchasing new construction properties for $10,000 that previously sold for $170,000 only 1.5-year prior! Everyone was scared to buy, the old-pro investors were losing their properties and portfolios, banks didn't want their properties, wealth was being transferred and lost, and it's still going on somewhat today (as of December 2009).

Regardless of what happens, there will still be renters and demand for affordable housing. Real estate is not a zero sum game like stocks. It is a commodity and will always retain a value, even if we lose the banks and they all go under, if you have title to a property, that's worth more than gold in my opinion. You have a physical tangible commodity with an address and a location on a map. As I write this article, gold is around $1,150 an ounce. I could take $30,000 and invest it in gold, and then the next day, lose it all if the prices go against my speculative trade.

Instead, I can take the $30,000 cash and buy 2 duplexes in the Cleveland real estate market, rehab them and hold for a cash flow or sell at a discount to an investor that doesn't want to deal with rehabs and contractors. The returns will surpass 100% annually, and the equity return will triple.

"Why am I telling you all this? What does it have to do with tips and traps in rental property investing?"

Because the biggest trap is; believing the media and what they say, and also what anyone else says about real estate. For instance, let's say you live in California and are interested in buying a couple cash flow properties in Cleveland. You mention it to a realtor or a friend who says you are crazy and will lose your shirt because Cleveland is a broke town with no renters or buyers. Doubt creeps into your mind and you decide to not even look into the matter and acquire the facts about the whole idea.

Meanwhile, another investor in the California market just purchased 4 large duplexes in a Cleveland neighborhood that are cash-flowing $1,100 per month per property, researched, interviewed and found a good manager and tradesman and plans on keeping the properties for a few years and then selling or refinancing.

I learned long ago that I have to get the facts about neighborhoods and rumors. I missed many great deals and opportunities because I thought a property was in a bad neighborhood or was just a bad deal, without taking the time and effort to look into it.

Myth#2: A property manager should know what to do at all times.

You are the employer. You are the entrepreneur. You must call several small property managers in your market. Interview them and ask them critical questions. If he or she will not cooperate with your interview or questions; move on, don't waste time. There are a lot of time bandits in this business. A time bandit is someone that will waste your precious wealth building time. You won't get it back.

If your property manager owns many rentals and investment properties in the market, don't use them. When advertising for tenants they will put the good tenants in their property, not yours.

Don't use a property manager for contracting and repairs. They will overcharge you and charge you ridiculous mark-ups.

Make sure the manager can rent Section 8. In some housing authorities(like Cleveland), you have to attend a landlord briefing class to accept or rent Section 8 Housing Choice Voucher Program.

If the property manager does not return phone calls or emails in a timely manner, this is a minor red flag of future behavior. Treat this as a light issue though, it may be that they are always busy talking and screening tenants or meeting tenants at properties, etc.

Myth#3: If I buy a house for $2,000 there is no way I can lose:

It will more than likely need over major repairs that may exceed it's value, have violations, possibly condemned and on the city demo list, delinquent taxes, title clouds, functionally obsolescent and in a really bad area.

In my observations, I noticed many out of areas investors buy these houses and then they were missing a few months later. The city demolished it. Cities are tired of real estate "intermediaries" that simply buy a "dump" for $1,000, sell to another investor for $5,000, then that investor sell it to another investor for $7,000, then that investor never gets around to doing the repairs because they didn't realize they were taking over a property that has a delinquent tax lien for $5,000 or more on it that is about to foreclose, is condemned, or the contractor ripped them off.

Then what? The city demolishes it. This is not just Cleveland; most cities are taking a strong proactive step towards this course of action.

Myth#4: Section 8 renters will destroy your property:

The key is to pre-screen your renter and your property manager will be doing this, unless you want to. I recommend Section 8 housing and renting. Most housing authorities are not giving out any new vouchers, so there are waiting lists and the ones that have good vouchers want to keep them. To destroy your property and make a mess may terminate their voucher for good.

Don't overlook cash tenants, once again, the key is to pre-screen your tenant and understand what events will cause you to fall into a tenant's game where they are controlling you. Of course, a good property manager should know all this....

Myth#5: Real Estate is no longer a local game because of the Internet

Real estate is local and will always be local; the Internet merely eliminates boundaries of information and access.

If you can't invest locally because of high prices, negative cash flow or negative emotional attachments, then going into another market makes sense. However, you must have a local team or "investor minded" expert with YOU from A to Z, no exceptions. A Realtor is not always going to look out for your best interest, and most Realtors do not understand real estate investing. Remember, a Realtor's main objective is to generate revenue though commissions.

Myth#6: Tenants Won't Pay Rent and There Aren't Any Good-Paying Renters In Low-Income Neighborhoods

Can you believe people actually believe this one?? There are more tenants out there than ever before. The problem is, some markets are flooded with shadow inventory, too many apartments and vacant foreclosed houses. BUT, as far as Cleveland is concerned, we have a SHORTAGE of apartment (quality) housing, which is pressuring the values and rents UP to a small degree...right now, and that COULD get stronger.

"I HAVE MY TENANT SCREENING PROCESS DOWN TO A SCIENCE. IT TAKES ME 4-6 WEEKS TO FIND A QUALITY, QUIET TENANT THAT WILL STAY FOR 2-5 YEARS AND PAY RENT ON TIME - ALL THE TIME - AND THIS IS IN THE CITY OF CLEVELAND, NOT THE SUBURBS"

It's really very simple, you have to have experience to know what to look for. It did take me some trial and error to pre-screen, and the key is to resist the urge to throw anybody in your unit that offers you a deposit and 1st month's rent!!! 4-6 WEEKS IS NOTHING!

Chapter 3

Finding Cash Flow and Equity

There are fantastic cash flow and equity deals in markets like Cleveland OH and other Midwest, Northeastern regions. I usually base an investment on its cash-on-cash return. Since an investor will be putting up 20% down-payment cash into a cash flow deal these days, I usually show what kind of return they will get per year on their cash investment. I normally don't deal with cap rates unless it's an all cash buyer or I'm rehabbing or selling an apartment building or anything over 5 units.

When buying a rehabbed, turnkey cash flow property this is what your typical numbers should look like. **These are actual turnkey deals I have sold to cash flow investors:**

Triplex Cash Flow Property (Leveraged):

MONTHLY BASIS.

PURCHASE PRICE	$73,000
20% DOWN PAYMENT	$14,600
PRINCIPAL LOAN AMOUNT	$58,400
PRINCIPAL & INTEREST PAYMENT (4.8%)	$306.40
TAXES	$143.14
INSURANCE	$60

P.I.T.I. PAYMENT   *$509.54*

EXPENSES:

WATER/SEWER	$60
PROPERTY MANAGEMENT	$100

TOTAL MONTHLY EXPENSES   *$669.54*

CASH FLOW:

UNTI 1 RENT	$575
UNTI 2 RENT	$575
UNIT 3 RENT	$400
TOTAL RENTS	*$1,550*
POSITIVE CASH FLOW:	*$880.46*
CASH ON CASH YIELD	*72%*
PROPERTY VALUE	$115,000
EQUITY	$56,500

Duplex Cash Flow Property (Leveraged):

MONTHLY BASIS.

PURCHASE PRICE	$59,500
20% DOWN PAYMENT	$11,900
PRINCIPAL LOAN AMOUNT	$47,600
PRINCIPAL & INTEREST PAYMENT (5.5%)	$270.27
TAXES	$134.83
INSURANCE	$50

P.I.T.I. PAYMENT	*$455.10*

EXPENSES:

WATER/SEWER	$60
PROPERTY MANAGEMENT	$100

TOTAL MONTHLY EXPENSES	*$615.10*

CASH FLOW:

UNTI 1 RENT	$550
UNTI 2 RENT	$510

TOTAL RENTS	*$1,060*
POSITIVE CASH FLOW:	*$444.90*
CASH ON CASH YIELD	45%
PROPERTY VALUE	$80,000
EQUITY	$32,400

Single-Family Cash Flow Property (Leveraged):

MONTHLY BASIS.

PURCHASE PRICE	$55,000
20% DOWN PAYMENT	$11,000
PRINCIPAL LOAN AMOUNT	$44,000
PRINCIPAL & INTEREST PAYMENT (5.8%)	$258.17
TAXES	$125.33
INSURANCE	$50

P.I.T.I. PAYMENT   *$433.50*

EXPENSES:

WATER/SEWER	$60
PROPERTY MANAGEMENT	$50

TOTAL MONTHLY EXPENSES   *$615.10*

CASH FLOW:

HOUSE RENT $825

POSITIVE CASH FLOW: *$209.90*
CASH ON CASH YIELD   23%

PROPERTY VALUE	$65,000
EQUITY	$21,000

You will find turnkey properties from investors that specialize in this such as myself.

You can also do it yourself and buy a fixer upper from either a local investor that will consult with you through from A to Z and let you use his/her contacts, or if you are in your backyard market you can do this all yourself.

I cannot delve into the mechanics of marketing and finding deals here, it's not the goal of this introductory book. If you have any questions just call me or text me.

ValleyWideInvestments.com

(216) 220-7027

Here are some things to make sure you are aware when analyzing the cash flow.

- Water and sewer bill costs.
- Property management fee structure (10% of gross or $50 per unit?)
- Taxes, and was there a re-assessment?
- Insurance costs, get multiple bids.
- Possible unit turnover costs.

Chapter 4

Financing

There are still non-owner occupied investor loans available if you meet the requirements. If you are buying a rehabbed duplex cash flow property, I don't suggest you use a mortgage broker/banker. You will save money by dealing with a local bank, regional bank, and credit union or community development source. When you contact the bank call their corporate headquarters and talk to an in-house loan agent to avoid paying brokers' fees. Don't use a mortgage broker, all they will do is take your file and application to the very same bank and wholesale the loan, after putting their points and fees on top.

A local bank knows the market and even though you may be 2000 miles away they would prefer that the property be in close proximity.

As of writing this in December 2009, lending criteria for a non-owner occupied investor loan is still the same. Roughly 20-30% down, verifiable documented income, good debt-to-income ratios, a good FICO credit score and you cannot own more than 4 properties in your name. Unfortunately, this eliminates a very large market share of investors that want to purchase.

"What other options are there if you cannot qualify for conventional financing?"

Hard Money

Hard money is a great way to leverage yourself into investment property if you have limited funds.

10-18% interest rates, 5-10 point rolled into loan, 3-6 month term, reserves, good credit and they are going to probably decline you if you can't prove your income or make you put up to 10-50% down. Most residential hard money companies fell off the planet when the market went south starting in mid-2008. A few big ones and small conservative local ones that only issued loans in their local market stayed the course. Basically, whoever is in the hard money lending business right now is going to be a strong lender and is well capitalized.

Cash Partner

You will pretty much have to split everything 50/50. It doesn't look to appealing when you lose 50% share on a residential property such as a $65,000 duplex cash flow property or single-family cash flow house.

Owner Financing

Great if you can find them. You will still need a down payment and the interest rate will be above market rates so that will hurt your cash flow a little bit.

Line of Credit

Hard to find, most were recalled in the past year. If you do have a line of credit and the rate is par with prime, it's great, use it now before the bank recalls it. Be careful of floating rates, if short-term interest rates rise, so will your line of credit finance rate.

Cash

Obviously the best way, you will receive a decent annual yield and equity return plus your cash will be secured in cash flowing "brick and mortar" real property, shielded from inflation.

Chapter 5

Inspection and Security

If you are buying a fixer upper, Be aware of repairs and problems in these areas:

- Furnaces and gas lines
- Water meter
- Water tanks
- Plumbing
- Electrical Panels and wiring system
- Roof layers, leaks, and gutters.
- Garage roof and door.
- Outlets, plugs and internal wiring (Knob and tube, aluminum, copper?)
- GFCI
- Exterior and interior doors
- Flu liner in chimney
- Windows and screens (Section 8 requires all screens and no chipped paint on windows)
- Chipped interior and exterior paint (Section 8 – no chipped paint anywhere)
- Light fixtures.
- Finished 3rd floor attic wiring and heating
- Do bedrooms have closets? (Section 8 prefers this)

Most important:

- Must have 2 bedrooms per unit for 2-3 unit properties.

- If it's a single family house, minimum 3 bedrooms.

- Avoid properties that have 1 coded bedroom and a converted dining room as the 2nd bedroom

- Avoid duplexes with a unit bathroom in the common area entrance.

- Do not buy properties with shared driveways.

- Make sure a vehicle can fit down the driveway and doesn't hit the house next door or your property.

- Make sure the property HAS a driveway.

- Pull a county plat map and make sure you know what you are getting before closing.

- If it's a financed deal, the lender will usually do a survey, making sure there are no encroachments or problems with the land boundaries.

Important Tip!

If you are dealing in low to middle income neighborhoods, make sure no one tampered with your electric utility meters outside if you just purchased it and are turning on the utilities in your name. Some utility companies will see that it was tampered with or someone "illegally" turned it on before you bought it or left it on (Typical in bank owned properties) and will charge you a fine up to $1,000 and some have the audacity to threaten you with criminal charges.

The duplex below was **not** one of my best deals. I purchased this small duplex in 2006, **and actually didn't realize it had no driveway until after closing.** Where is the tenant going to park? "On street" parking is the tenant's only choice and they will most likely move on to another rental that has a driveway.

That's what I thought, but it actually had no problem renting, although the rents were just a little bit lower than the current sub-market rents. I attribute this to the location and neighborhood. It is a quiet street in Cleveland. Some of you reading this may be thinking that only an idiot would miss something as obvious as a driveway, but you could make the same mistake too, I had bought many properties before this one, so it can happen to anyone.

This property also had a converted dining room in each unit to make it a 2 bedroom per unit property.

Chapter 6

Security

This is a very important subject matter and applies to all markets and neighborhoods.

Secure your property before or immediately after closing. I usually do it before closing, before I even start a purchase I make sure I know everything about a property from the plat maps, to the legal description and physical condition. I am used to taking the risk of securing a property before I take title. However, please be aware that it is not technically allowed.

The price of metals has a lot to do with your property rehab cost and theft risk potential.

When the price of metals goes up, so do my thefts, break-ins and vandalism on vacant properties. I am writing this section in January 2010 and copper is almost back to it's 2008 high. If you follow my advice and security strategies, you will hedge your risk a thousand-fold.

Illustration: High grade copper commodities cash price chart October 27, 2017.

Source: United Futures Trading, Inc.

Week of:10/27/2017 O=3.1450 H=3.1870 L=3.0740 C=3.0935 V=551900

10/27/2017 C=3.0935 -.0580 O=3.1450 H=3.1870 L=3.0740

RSI 65.38 20.00 80.00

Volume 551900.00 Open Interest 310694.00

Created with SuperCharts by Omega Research ® 1997

If you are buying a fixer upper vacant duplex or single family house in the city, or any kind of residential property, DO NOT BOARD IT UP. Don't board your property up, and if someone already boarded it up (such as a bank or possibly the City), **remove them immediately**. Here's why:

- It attracts thieves and makes them want to break in to steal any remaining metals to scrap.

- City inspectors take notice and will violate the property.

- The contractor that installed them more than likely didn't do it right, thus the boards are ineffective.

- Becomes an eyesore.

- It's a waste of money.

My Recommended Property Security Plan

- Switch utilities into your name before closing, mainly electricity. Use a LLC or corporation to open the utility accounts and make sure you have an EIN# ready because they will need that.

- Install an alarm system, specifically audible sirens that are tripped by motion detectors AND magnetic strips on first floor entrances and egresses. Make sure a siren speaker is installed on the inside and on the exterior. Make sure the exterior siren horn is at least 15-20 feet high on the property, close to roof or second unit.

- Turn 3 lights on in the lower unit or first floor. A bathroom light, a lamp in the living room and the common area hallway light. Leave them on always or use timers.

- Install cheap paper shades from home depot on every single window on the lower unit or first floor, including the doors if they have windows. Close them all.

- Screw the front door shut from inside. You will only use the side or rear door.

- Replace bulbs on front porch light and side/rear entrance exterior lights, leave on 24 hrs. a day, 7 days a week.

- Install a motion detector floodlight in the rear/side portion of the house. Have it set to remain on for 15 minutes when detecting motion.

- Install a security sign outside so people know it's alarmed (usually comes with security installation).

- Install new deadbolt locksets on all exterior doors.

- Put a radio on in one of the bedrooms or living room. Preferably news channel, Or use a real TV.

This type of alarm system will cost $250 to $375. I pay my alarm guy in Cleveland $375 per property. It does not report to the Police (costs more and is not needed). When tripped, an extremely loud siren goes off inside and outside. It stays on for 15 minutes then automatically resets. If it still detects motion after 15 minutes, it will keep tripping.

When this alarm goes off, it wakes up the entire block(s), someone will call the Police and the thief will not stay around. The alarm circuit box is usually hidden somewhere in the property, with a 24 hour back-up battery. Even if they find and destroy the keypad, it will still work. The thief would have to find the circuit box, and we usually hide that well, either in a closet or in the attic, or somewhere in the basement not easily found.

What all this does it makes it look like someone lives there. A thief is looking for a vacant house he can rip the copper plumbing out of and scrap for money, or a metal sink, or anything metallic he/she can steal and scrap.

When I stopped using boards, I stopped having break-ins on my vacant properties.

This is not a 100% protection guarantee, but will greatly reduce a break-in until you find another renter or while you are rehabbing your property.

Does all this scare you?

Are you thinking that this only applies to "war zones" or bad neighborhoods? Sorry, it's everywhere. Metal prices have been so volatile in the past few years and there are thieves everywhere, it is happening in the rural areas, suburbs and urban infill areas. If you follow my security procedure you will reduce a break-in significantly. It has to be done right, though.

Total cost will be around $500 - $600

When do you want to board up a house?

The only time I would board a house up is if it is rehabbed and in good condition, in a risky neighborhood and you absolutely cannot risk a break in and you don't want to pay utilities to keep power and gas on. So, when an inspector comes by and demands to get inside for an inspection for possible violations, you won't have to worry because it is rehabbed.

To gain access your property manager or associate will have to bring an electric battery powered drill gun with a flat head and a hex head drill bit to take the side door board off.

By the way, the cost to board up a house/duplex properly is going to cost approximately the same as my security procedure outlined previously.

Here's how to board up a property correctly:

- Use ¾ thick inch plywood.

- Use 2 reinforced 2x4 shunts from interior.

- Screw board in from inside and tighten against reinforced so you don't damage your window coil by screwing board into that.

- Use a combination of hex screws interlaced with Philips and flat heads for doorway boards. Most thieves will only have a one drill bit with them.

- Paint boards white or off-white on the exterior. *See illustration below:*

The method is correct but the boards are misplaced. There should be no seam or gap in the middle where 2 boards meet.

The correct way would be to use 2 exact sized boards per window, snap them into the inseam frame depression from outside and then secure and tighten them with the reinforced 2x4 as shown below. Of course, make sure the window is open.

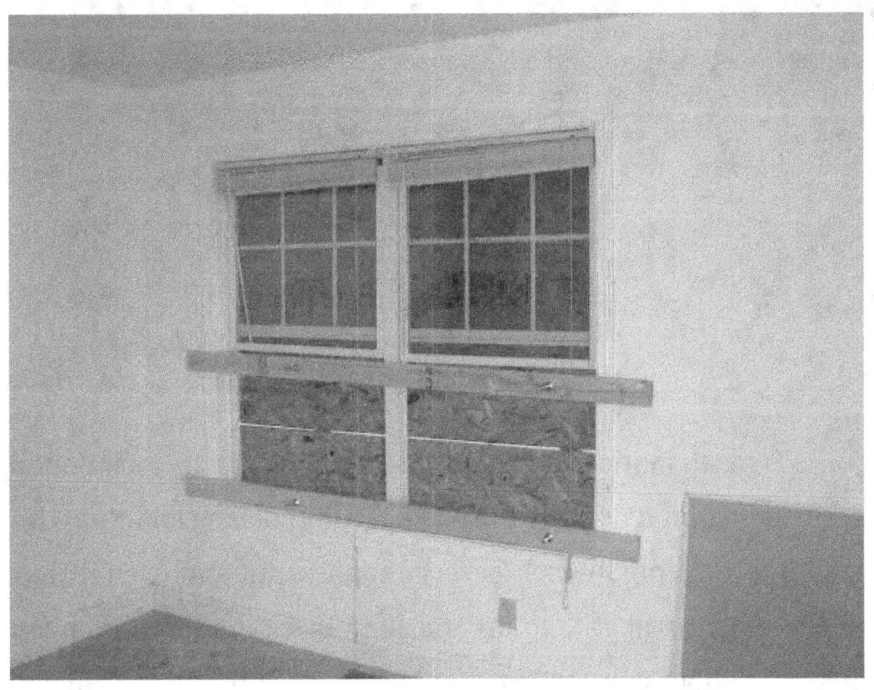

This is an incorrect board up.

The front door is done correctly, but not the windows. See how the top window coil is showing. A thief can use a crow bar to crack open the board and break in. Also, the boards should be individual PER WINDOW. You cannot have a seam or gap, and you cannot use one big board to cover all the windows, plus, look how horrible this looks!

Typical motion detector floodlight correctly positioned and installed on a duplex. I use the flexible plastic conduit with metal interior lining which is very tough to cut and even if they tried, the light will still go on and illuminate the thief scumbag while a neighbor can see him/her, and hopefully call the Police.

"It's always good to have glass block windows. Easy maintenance and security."

When you <u>must</u> "winterize" your property:

If you just rehabbed a house or it's already rehabbed but you now have a vacancy, please follow these instructions if the climate is cold or will be approaching freezing temperatures. You must winterize the unit/property or risk losing your plumbing systems, which will incur a possible couple thousand dollars in repairs. **Remember that, " Busted Pipes Equals Busted Check Book"**

- Open all lines at the sink, faucets, bathtub and utility sink.

- Go into basement and shut off the Main Water Valve on the city pipe.

- If you have a secondary shut-off valve, turn that one off next.

- Drain out the water tanks by opening the water valves, let the water drain into basement drain. It won't be that much water.

- All sinks and spouts should be hissing a little bit of air leftover at this point. **Leave all valves and spouts open.**

- Purchase one jug of standard anti-freeze and pour a little bit in your sink on second floor and bathtub.

- Flush toilets to flush out remaining water, and then pour some antifreeze into bowl and reservoir. It's ok if there is some water remaining in toilet bowl, the anti-freeze will protect it.

This is a copper water line (Surrounded in insulation) going up to the basement ceiling where the secondary water shut-off is (blue knob), make sure that is shut off as well in case the city valve malfunctions. The rest of the plumbing conduits are CPVC.

One way to minimize your plumbing being ruptured by cold temperatures is to use the PEX flexible plumbing lines. They are made of materials that don't easily break from the water expanding and contracting pressures caused by freezing temperatures. It is more expensive, but if your lines burst due to freezing temperatures and a negligent property manager, it could cost much more to repair it.

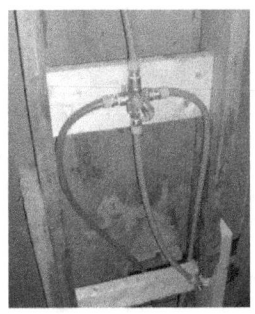

Chapter 7

Contractors

If you are doing a fixer upper, here are the tips and traps to be completely aware of when dealing with local or out of state repair crews. Do not trust any contractor ever, and always hold them accountable.

General contractor

When you need to do repairs and you are out of the area, you will need to use a contractor because they have a crew ready to go and will oversee the work of subcontractors they hire or specialized tradesman in electric, HVAC, plumbing, roofing, etc.

Sub-contractors:

Use these skilled tradesmen when you are local and can oversee their work, it will be cheaper than a contactor (usually).

Handyman / cheap labor

Use the general skilled handyman if you are local and can baby-sit him/her. The labor will be (has to be) cheap and you will be accompanying the handyman to acquire supplies or purchase them over phone through the pro-desk at Home Depot or Lowe's.

Down-payment

You shouldn't have to put anything down at all if you sign a solid contract with a real contractor; they have their own lines of commercial credit to use to get materials and work started fast. But those guys are usually more expensive. So when dealing with smaller contractors to save money, a lot of them don't have the capital or don't want to spend the capital to front materials for you the investor. They have been "burned" too and are just as concerned as you are about getting paid for their work and services.

Most contractors will try to get half down and some actually have enough nerve to ask for the whole amount of the job upfront. Don't do any of this. Some of you reading will be thinking, "Who the hell would do something so stupid?" Unfortunately, some do, they just want to trust someone and that's it.

You should never put more than 10% down in my opinion, if you do have to put anything down. If the contractor needs your money to buy supplies, offer to have the contractor go to the supply store, get the materials and have the pro desk call you and take a credit card over the phone once you verify the supplies the contractor is ordering.

Otherwise, I suggest you not use a contractor that asks for half down and explains they need this so they can buy the materials to get started. Move on and find someone else, there are plenty of crews out there that need work!

Nothing bothers me more than a contractor telling me what I have to do in order to give him my money. If a contractor says I have to pay his prices with no negotiations, sign their contract that protects them and give them 25% down, I tell them to get lost.

Do not beg a contractor or tradesman to take your money, that's essentially what you are doing if you have to wait on them or do everything their way. Sound crazy? It is. Many times I found myself in a position where I had jobs ready to go and I couldn't find a contractor to do them because they wouldn't come down a few hundred dollars on the price, or they wanted 25% down instead of 10% down or they wouldn't sign MY contract instead of their absurd contract. I am talking about $15,000 jobs. They would rather not take my $15,000 over minor details that I just described. I'm sure this all makes sense to a contractor reading this, but from my point of view, I'm the employer and the contractor is killing future business by dealing in this manner.

You are paying them your hard earned cash, and are employing them to perform a service of which you do not know if they will perform 100%. The risk is on the investor; so do not deal with contractors that say "It's my way or the highway."

In addition, you need the contractor to get you an itemized quotation upfront before negotiations (not a contract) for repairs. You want to know where exactly your dollars are going to be spent. Vague or fuzzy quotes means the contractor is usually going to look for ways to skim or adjust things "under your nose" and make more money off you, and more than likely you will have overages or problems with him/her.

Example of how things should be itemized. When someone says, the total cost for a completely new rental grade kitchen is $5,500, make him or her break it down, then you will see what makes more sense. The numbers below are normally what I can get an entire kitchen rehabbed for in the city, a large sized eat-in kitchen. If I use a sub-contractor or my general handyman that I have to baby-sit, the cost will go down significantly.

Kitchen Rehab Section (Material and labor charges I pay)

- New counters. Home depot. Beige: $300
- All new ceramic tile flooring: $200
- All new low grade cabinets. Wood. $1,200
- New plumbing attachments: $50
- 3 new outlets. 2 GFCI's. 3 switches: $80
- Metallic sink and faucet attachment $225
- New light fixture: $25

TOTAL: **$2,100.00**

You should have a break down for every section of the quote. Bathrooms, plumbing, electrical, doors and windows, roof, painting and patchwork, carpet, flooring, etc.

Long Distance Accountability

So how do you pay the contractor if you are not in town to verify repairs are done?

There have been so many scams I have seen and been victim of when I first started; this is where you have to be careful. Let's say it's a $20,000 rehab and you put 10% down ($2,000) and the first phase was all new plumbing and water tanks.

Have the contractor take detailed photos and email them to you, in which you then mail the next draw so the contractor can move onto the kitchens and bathrooms rehab.

However, how do you know it's really YOUR house and YOUR plumbing the pictures represent?

Warning signs:

- Close up pictures of new material and no background to reveal it's your house they may be snapping a photo of someone else's plumbing or a new water tank at Home Depot.

- Fuzzy photos or half-taken with blurs and blockages.

- No photos at all!

- When you bought the property you had someone go in and take detailed photos such as the realtor or prospective property manager. Do the contractor photos match the pre-rehab photos?

When you call the contractor up and explain that the photos need to be re-taken, he or she will usually complain that "they would never screw you over and that they can assure the water tanks and plumbing were installed, so please send me my money, I have a good reputation around here and you can call my references."

At this point you will need to ask (politely but with some hard nosed attitude) for him/her to re-take the photos and that this is a very serious business for you and you need reassurance the repairs are being done on your house.

If the contractor refuses to co-operate or even if they take several days to get the proper accountable photos, have a property manager that you should already be interviewing or working with physically go there and verify, then cancel your contract and find someone else immediately. There is a high risk they didn't do the work, or even if they did, you will not want to work with a contractor that won't co-operate with you. You are losing time and money because of the contractor's delays. You may lose $2,000, in which you will want to then file a police report or file a claim in civil court. You will need an attorney's assistance.

Here are some serious warning signs and red flags of a bad contractor or sub-contractor:

- Never answers phone. (I really hate this one)

- Lies to you, never shows up on specified times and dates.

- Makes promises that are never met.

- Keeps promising repairs but keeps missing deadlines.

- No show, no call.

- "Scatterbrain"

- Doesn't have a real email address (uses their girlfriend or mothers email address)

- Does not have reliable transportation.

- **Doesn't follow instructions** or **argues with you**.

- Displays a carefree attitude and doesn't care about your deadline or goal.

- Thinks they are the boss and can do the work on their own schedule, such as, "I'll get to it next week because I am finishing up another job, DON'T WORRY IT WILL GET DONE." (Never gets done...)

- Something in your "gut" is saying not to use the contractor after talking on the phone, etc. They don't sound professional on the phone, slurs or speak incoherently.

- Cannot deliver a quote or contract on a real letterhead in a professional manner.

Other Tips When Dealing With Contractors:

- Ask to see past project photos.

- Ask for some local references.

- Go to the county website CLERK OF COURTS and see if their last name show up on any criminal dockets or civil dockets. Have they been sued, arrested for theft, burglary, and felonies, ASSAULT??

- Ask the property manager if they know anything about your new contractor you are checking out.

- Cross reference their company name (LLC or Corp) with the SECRETARY OF STATE WEBSITE and see if it really exists; and if so, check to see if their name is on the corporate documents, or who the statutory agent is.

- "Google" their name or company name.

- Find their personal residence through the COUNTY AUDITOR PROPERTY website and keep for future reference in the event you get ripped off.

- Before they start the job require and request a copy of the Drivers License, Insurance and Bond.

- Make sure they have contractors insurance minimum $1,000,000 and if applicable, their contractors' license. Note, some jurisdictions do not require a general contractors' license.

- Do not become friends with your contractor, subs or handyman personnel ever. Keep it all business. And don't tell them your budget or bottom line. Do not tell them your investment or what you paid for the property. It is none of their business. **When a contractor starts asking questions about how much money you will make or is verbally estimating your profit right in front of your face, consider dropping them right there, seriously**.

You want to keep copies and records of all the above in case there is a tort, malfeasance or breach of contract. You want to know where their statutory agent is (if they have one), their personal address for sending summons, etc. Information can be a great form of leverage in negotiations.

Track all your expenses on a spreadsheet:

For every cash flow property you buy or rehab, use a spreadsheet to track all expenses, especially when rehabbing. Keep all related receipts in an envelope solely dedicated to that property that match up with a dedicated Excel spreadsheet. Then when tax time comes it will be easy to access your records.

Make sure the contractor is keeping materials and waste in a container. They usually cost $200-$250 for a 2 week period in most cities. Make sure they haul it away after filling it up. Keep in mind some container companies will charge you extra if you over-fill the container.

Below is a violation notice I got from the City of Cleveland when I made the mistake of keeping the waste container in the driveway too long. There was a parade coming up so the "housing specialists" walked the street looking for things to violate. I also had 2 wrappers in the yard. Sometimes these city officials "enjoy" writing tickets on landlords and property owners, it makes them feel good knowing they have a little bit of power.

CITY OF CLEVELAND
DIVISION OF ENVIRONMENT

VIOLATION NOTICE

1925 ST. CLAIR AVENUE
CLEVELAND, OHIO 44114
PHONE: 216/664-2300

NAME: Cleveland Brothers Llc
ADDRESS: PO Box 1254
CITY, STATE, ZIP: Medina Ohio 44258

DATE: 5/29/09
PHONE:

VL	M	DIST
S	C	CT
D	O	W

YOU ARE HEREBY NOTIFIED AS: ☑ OWNER ☐ AGENT ☐ OCCUPANT

KEEP CLEVELAND CLEAN AND FREE OF RATS

OF THE PREMISES LOCATED AT: 900 Riple

TO COMPLY WITH THE CHECKED ITEMS BELOW BY THE FOLLOWING DATE: ⌐ DATE 6-5-09 ⌐

RIGHT TO APPEAL TO THE BOARD OF ZONING APPEALS

- ☒ 203.07 Provide sufficient approved containers for refuse, waste
- ☒ 203.07 Keep all refuse, waste covered and confined in approved containers
- ☒ 203.07 Remove all waste, litter from the ground
- ☐ 205.02 Abate the nuisance of animals causing odors, unsanitary conditions
- ☐ 211.02 Abate the nuisance of rodents, insects or vermin
- ☐ 211.02 Abate the rodent, vermin harborage
- ☐ 551.04 Discontinue placing solid waste out for pick-up prior to noon on the day preceding scheduled pick-up

RIGHT TO APPEAL TO THE COMMISSIONER OF ENVIRONMENT

- ☒ 209.01 Abate the nuisance of refuse and/or junk, garbage
- ☒ 209.01 Abate the nuisance of tires, offal, and/or other waste
- ☒ 209.01 Abate the nuisance of ct grass in excess of 8" in height
- ☒ 209.01 Abate the nuisance of noxious weeds
- ☐ 209.01 Abate the nuisance of animal waste
- ☐ 209.01 Abate the nuisance of stagnant water

INSPECTOR: Bob Russ PHONE: 664 7407

FAILURE TO COMPLY MAY RESULT IN FURTHER ACTION UNDER PENALTY IMPOSED BY CODE

RECEIVED BY

C of E 56-117 9/2005

57

Some Final Suggestions

- It pays to be paranoid and get everything in writing, especially when dealing with city contractors.

- Be consistent in this business or become non-existent.

- Never trust a realtor when you are making an offer as a dual agency on one of their listings, remember they will look out for the Seller's best interest even if it is a bank, they will hide some facts or mislead you sometimes.

- Real estate is a commodity, it can be rented and sold as long as people have money, jobs, families, and when there are no more jobs, you have government assistance to pay you rent money.

- NEVER let your emotions affect your real estate investment activities and decisions. Stay objective and un-attached. Remain calm and focused when speaking with property managers, contractors, sellers and tenants and ESPECIALLY the court room judge when evicting.

- In low-income areas, don't take tenants' credit scores too seriously; be more focused about their job income source, references and their second last landlord. Especially for Section 8 tenants, the government is paying the rent. Just make sure they have a job and/or income source, as Section 8 usually requires the tenant to front a small fraction of the rent.

- Make sure you check with your local municipal rental laws for who has to pay the water and sewer bill. Sometimes in properties greater that 1 unit, the Owner must pay the water and sewer unless the property is sub-metered or individually metered.

- You can usually verify title with most online county recorders office websites, for free.

- Before buying a property, call the Building and Housing department for that particular county and make sure there are no violations on the property, or if it has been condemned.

- **DO NOT "SCREW" PEOPLE OVER IN THIS BUSINESS**, it will come back to hurt you down the road, <u>guaranteed</u>. If a tradesman/contractor does their job right, pay them. If you commit to buying a property, follow through. If for some reason you can't follow through, then call the seller or agent right away and let them know. Don't pull the old "disappearing act" because that will discredit you so fast and you will make enemies. Don't sneak around people's backs and double talk. Don't lie to people in this business, it is easy to spot lies, and you will be discredited very fast. Keep your integrity high, be transparent and just be honest with people in this business, they will respect you for it, and every local market is a SMALL market.

Chapter 7

Coming Trends

I don't have a crystal ball; however, based on my experience and observations in the marketplace, I believe, in my opinion, there are some things that I can say with personal confidence have a high probability of happening.

"A Shadow REO Inventory"

As I write this in January 2010, it is a known fact that many banks holding back on foreclosures, defaulted mortgages and paper, and have been doing loan modifications and extensions with hundreds of thousands of property owners. This has created an accumulated foreclosure inventory in some markets that is quite scary. This accumulation hasn't even reached the REO stage yet. If one takes this into consideration, the housing problems will not go away for a few more years.

This is great if you are an investor, but will hamper you if you plan on flipping to retail buyers, especially when the Tax Credit expires this year (2010)

Once again, the best strategy is to buy, secure equity and hold for cash flow.

Bulk REO Trends

Another trend I see is banks and government entities are looking to sell their REO properties on the private auction block or sell their properties in a bulk pool to one buyer.

This isn't always great for the small local investor like me. I source my deals by buying REO bank owned properties direct. I like REO because it is clean title and taxes are paid up to date. It's a clean transaction, no seller to deal with, very little human interaction; communications are usually done by email, no title problems, no tax delinquencies, etc.

However; the banks are starting to put their properties in private auction blocks more and more. Another trend is selling the pool of properties as-is with a quit claim deed, so the one buyer that purchases 50 properties from one bank assumes all title and tax problems and delinquencies. Typically a deal like this will sell for $500 per house. This really kills values locally and ruins it for sellers with quality-rehabbed properties.

Cities and counties are buying vacant and bank owned properties.

I thought it was bad enough when competing against pro-investors, now I have the entire city as competition. Cleveland recently acquired several millions in funding by offering bonds, to buy and profit off cheap, vacant properties.

This is happening in many cities according to some of the buzz I hear. Sometimes they demolish the properties that are no good. This isn't that bad, because their goal is to get the ones that need demolished, but I am seeing the city buy "nice" properties too.

Inflation / Deflation?

Based upon how much printed money is swishing around out there in banks and bailouts, it only makes sense one or the other will occur in some form. So, let's see how each one will affect real estate investing.

Inflation:

How does inflation affect a real estate investor?

- Property values will rise, in a strange way.

- If you are acquiring financing with high interest rates, your cash flow will suffer or be wiped out to a negative.

- Rents will rise.

- Utility costs will rise.

- Commodity costs will rise.

- Investors holding properties with adjustable rate mortgages will go into distress if they cannot cover the added debt service.

"That's why it is important you buy now, while rates are still low and properties can be bought relatively cheap with equity and positive cash flow."

No one knows what is going to happen, but do not rely on the economy to invest in real estate. People made millions during the last Depression and in the recent recession, and many will continue to create immense wealth as others stay on the sidelines or are too scared to do anything. What has happened before will happened again, so this isn't new stuff, no matter what the media says.

Deflation

Many economists believe this is much worse than inflation. There are pros and cons, but if you have some cash on hand it is extremely opportunistic for you to buy property at rock bottom prices. A prolonged economic deflation is essentially a Depression. They usually last 3-7 years, or longer. It is a de-leveraging cycle whereby banks and consumers begin realizing losses and writing down loans, causing asset values to shrink, ever further, and demand falls, and consumers begin saving cash.

- Costs will decrease in general.

- Cost of conventional loans will be extremely low, but lending will be very restricted, if not non-existent.

- Assets such as real estate, stocks and commodities will lose further value.

- Consumers spend less and borrow less, creating more pressure on declining prices.

- Unemployment remains relatively high.

- Vacancies increase in the commercial sector and even apartments.

- Stagnant property prices can linger for years.

Even if there are some major changes to the American Economy still coming, please remember that most of them have already happened before, and nothing is really that different. There is nothing holding anyone back from real estate in any market cycle, the only thing that matters is if your strategy is coherent with the current market. Like many gurus always say; you can make money in a good or bad market. I personally like the bad markets because of the lower prices and my cash offers get accepted more.

In a good, heated real estate market, Sellers don't care about cash, they just want the highest price and they usually get it if the house is rehabbed and/or in a decent neighborhood. I speak from experience.

Affordable Housing / Low Income Housing

There is an alarming shortage of low income and affordable housing and apartments developing in almost every major U.S. market.

Because of the recession and frozen lending markets of the recent past, developers were not building new apartments and housing for low income and affordable income tenants. This has created a shortage of supply in the market. In addition, the L.I.H.T.C. (LOW INCOME HOUSING TAX CREDITS) market has also come to a virtual stop. Without those credits being purchased by investors (which was mostly banks), developers have not been able to finance their affordable housing projects or re-developments.

It is projected that the "echo-boomer" and millennial generation (the baby boomers' children) are the ones that will comprise the majority of the apartment renter market into the next 15 years. We are now in a time where incomes are lower and affordable housing is needed more than ever. This market demand is HUGE and will only get bigger. An entire book can be written about this.

When inflation strikes and rents go up and the cost of living rises again, the owners of affordable apartment buildings, triplexes, duplexes and singles will benefit the most as they receive the value-added rents, income and property values. Millionaires will be made. It is a tremendous opportunity.

On a side note, if we experience another Deflationary wave, then you have to go into buying mode.

(Read these articles related to the shortage of low income/affordable housing. Source Multifamilyexecutive.com)

- http://www.multifamilyexecutive.com/table-of-contents/multifamily%20executive/2009/August.aspx

- http://www.multifamilyexecutive.com/affordable-housing/call-to-action.aspx

- http://www.multifamilyexecutive.com/affordable-housing/vicious-cycle.aspx

You can only benefit if you start investing and buying now before rents go up and properties get more expensive.

Here is what your cash flow looks like when mortgage interest rates rise, which is "predicted" to occur when inflation rears it's ugly head any day now. Remember there was a time in our country when rates were in the 15-18% prime. For the example, let's assume rates rise quickly to 9.5%

Duplex Cash Flow Property:

MONTHLY BASIS.

PURCHASE PRICE	$59,500
20% DOWN PAYMENT	$11,900
PRINCIPAL LOAN AMOUNT	$47,600
PRINCIPAL & INTEREST PAYMENT (9.5%)	*$400.25*
TAXES	$134.83
INSURANCE	$50
P.I.T.I. PAYMENT	*$585.08*

EXPENSES:

WATER/SEWER	$60
PROPERTY MANAGEMENT	$100
TOTAL MONTHLY EXPENSES	*$745.08*

CASH FLOW:

UNTI 1 RENT	$550
UNTI 2 RENT	$510
TOTAL RENTS	*$1,060*
POSITIVE CASH FLOW:	*$314.92*
CASH ON CASH YIELD	45%
PROPERTY VALUE	$80,000
EQUITY	$32,400

You still have a positive cash flow, but you lost almost $130 per month or $1,559.76 per year. Rates are still low, but it's my opinion and belief they will rise when the Fed decides it must be done, and I think they will go high. You want to get in while conventional money is still cheap.

"I encourage you to study my website and consider one of my properties. I have a good track record; can provide solid references of real investors that purchased from me. I add and contribute real value and want long-term business relationships."

www.valleywideinvestments.com

About The Author

"I started my real estate investment business as an owner-operator in the City of Cleveland, buying up cheap foreclosed singles, duplexes, triplexes and small apartment buildings. I would typically refurbish and sell to an investor and I learned a lot from hands-on experience.

As of 2017 I have done over 356 properties, mostly in Cleveland, but also in Phoenix, Dayton, Akron and Flint. I am currently involved in only 2 markets and enjoy helping others achieve their goals in real estate through my special niche property programs located at www.valleywideinvestments.com.

If you have any questions please call or email. I appreciate any and all feedback on whether or not this information has been of any value to you.

Thank you for your positive Amazon review if this information was helpful to you personally.

If you are interested in purchasing a turnkey or fixer-upper cash flow property that will give you up to an 20% annual yield on your money, contact me today and let's talk.

Valleywide Investments, LLC.
14837 Detroit Ave #202
Lakewood, OH 44107
(216) 220-7027
Info@valleywideinvestments.com
www.ValleywideInvestments.com

A Cleveland Duplex Purchased For $36,500
and It Cash Flows $1,300 per Month.